SINK IN INK

PALAK RAJPUT

Made with ♥ on the Notion Press Platform
www.notionpress.com

Time waits for none, and winds never require directions. It depends on us, how we use time and turn winds in our favor. We can make the best use of our leisure time by reading books, they are the lighthouse of wisdom and enlighten our souls. I would like to dedicate this book to my Family members and Books that I have come across! Reaching the height of Writing a Book, beginning with the journey of reading books would have been incomplete without the opportunities that I was provided with, and the failures which blocked my path, I would like to thank them for making me bolder and widening my viewpoint.

The words of a book always inspire, console, heal and nourish us. In my perspective, Library is the ultimate source to beat boredom and loneliness. A book always provides a unique perspective to carry ahead and live with! Each page increases our thirst for reading the book ahead and discovering something alluring in it. Flipping each page attracts our interest towards it by teaching us lessons about life, and the value of time. Henceforth, I'd like to thank all the books that I have read, and my family members for the faith they had in me as it eventually helped me in writing "SINK IN INK."

"A reader lives a thousand lives before he dies..... The man who never reads lives only one.

Contents

Preface

Dear Readers,

Reading and Writing have enthralled me ever since I was in Grade 5. I started writing Poems and Articles, officially when I was in Grade 7, and I finally started getting my work published in the Media Corners of The Hindustan Times and The Times of India Newspaper. I always dreamt of getting my Poetry Debut Book Published! I am thankful to my institution, as it has furnished me with numerous opportunities to showcase my talent. I want to bring to your notice that you must not let your passion wither away! You must always allow it to spark a fire in you as you're Fireworks! Passion must be followed, not just for building up a career, but rather because it revives a tired soul, acts as sleep on a red-eye, and Writing is as gracious as Soda on a Hot Summer Day and like a blanket in winter. Writing allows you to pen down your emotions. At times, we can't be expressive about things, and trust me "It's okay not to be Okay!" I invite you all to drench into the sanctity of my poetic verses as The words Unspoken, have been Spoken here! Possibly, we're on the same page readers! Let's Sink into the Ink, and take a deep dive into pure, uttered, and silenced emotions.

Prologue

The book **"Sink In Ink"** revolves around various themes and emotions such as Contentment, Excitement, Passion, Failures, Depression, Anxiety, Loneliness, Tears, Motivation Patriotism, etc.

Various bonds and relationships have been significantly highlighted such: Mother-Daughter, Football-Footballer, Teacher-Student, Tiranga-Indian, Mother Nature-Children, Family-Child, Failures-Success....and the list shall endlessly continue. The bond that a writer shares with her diary and pen is immeasurable in this world. If you feel nobody is there by your side, pick a theme, read a poem, and talk to her in your verses, she will never judge, get ready as your heart will sink in it.

If you're a Football Fan, I highly recommend you to read Oh, Football!, and for a Mother's Day Special nothing can be better than "The Roar of an Offspring's Heart!"

Find your interest, tighten your seatbelts, take a deep breath, and get ready to Sink In Ink with me!

1. The Highest Height

From mornings to night,

From darkness to light,

Life brings out new reasons to develop fright!

Although the future seems to be bright!

I'm holding on emotions really, tight..

Yesterday, i broke out in a fight,

Unpleasant; was the sight.

As in front of me, was my own timid side!

Although the reason was neither too wide,

I was just willing to hide!

No! I'm not afraid of heights

I love to gaze at flying kites.

So, I'd like to be on the other side,

Probably glancing at the highest tide

And being her guide!

New; will be the view, and

beautiful; will be the hue

Also, I'll not have to stand in a queue,

As in the Blue World, I'll be the new crew!

I promise, I'll tighten all the loose screws.

In my imagination, this is all I drew!

While, sipping brew.

As quite long, the grass grew!

With plenty of light,

The sight must be; bright!
As, I want to climb the Highest height!
And, fetch myself the best sight,
And, fetch myself the best sight!

2. A New Dusk!

With teary eyes and
heavy hearts,
2022 year has come to an end,
pretty fast...
time is what we have spent,
Spending a couple of cents,
moving out with family and friends,
Spending hours in the bright rays of the sun,
We often spent evenings, having fun.
We even played with toy guns!
Yes! We enjoyed a 'ton'
But, time and winds wait for none,
So, here's another year,
to make us run,
and have fun under the sun!

3. Oh, Football!

You start to roll,
when a player gives you a call
you often make me fall,
for I'm not too tall
I took you out of my hall,
but Oh, Football!
You always miss my call...
you often take my test,
never let me rest,
but I still try to perform my best
whenever I chase you, you quickly run
What do you find in it; 'Fun'?
I know, I'm as slow as a turtle,
and probably that's my biggest hurdle,
Whenever I try to chase,
you appear to me, like a mirror maze,
you always make me run,
I guess a 'ton'
I know I'm shy,
but I still try,
rather than pouring out a hefty 'cry'
Although I don't know how to play, without any shame,
I have started playing, as you are an addicting game,
You know what?

I have spent sleepless nights,
thinking about our endless friendly, fights,
exactly running from left to right
do you think that's a wonderful sight?
if yes, then you're genuinely not right.
Can I request you not to often make me fall?
Also, please stop missing my call
and be my friend 'Oh, Football!

4. Climate Action

*Sands of time have
rendered fear,
and because of our
callous demeanor,
lands have become
totally clear,
while the ethereal spirit of forest
has become something
humans are unable to bear.
Blue sky is now, no longer clear
and that's what I fear!
So we must get a control
on the carbon print,
else everything will
completely wilt,
Ocean's acidification
can be clearly seen,
But, being mean,
no one is ready to
make it clean.
Corals are bleaching, and
plastic has started leaching.
Lands are flooding or drying,
and glaciers have started melting every time......*

If it continues...
we'll not be able to survive,
but we have a solution and
that's stop pollution !
So let's reduce and reuse,
rather than adopting the ideology : 'REFUSE'
and fewer the use of plastic
to get rid of its ill drastics.
Let's say no to cutting trees,
and reduce emissions
so that everyone is able to breathe,
And step ahead,
Because
"Everyone is living on this planet,
as if we have another one to go."
But..
We'll know the worth of water,
Once the well will be dry...

5. Oh, Tears!

You are what I often wear,
you don't let me up a gear!
I know my courage is timid and mere,
and yes, you are what I often fear!
Though, your sound is what I don't let people hear,
my demeanor is what you often tear,
you are what I don't like to wear, and at times,
my eyes are not worth wearing you 'tears,'
because, Oh,dear! you are my biggest fear...

6. An Owe to you Downpour!

Oh, Rain!
You are solely holy,
When things make me feel pissed,
You are what I often miss!
Judgemental: you've never been,
A selfless friend in you is what I have often seen!
Thank you for crying with me,
Thank you for mourning with me,
Thank you for drenching me in your sanctity,
Thank you for letting me know, that it's not only me who is broken,
Thank you for not judging me,
Thank you for letting me know it's alright not to be okay!
Thank you for accepting me, the way I am...
Thank you for descending, and sitting by my side!
Thank you for allowing me to lean on your shoulder when I was all alone!
Thank you for listening to me for hours without any complaints!
Thank you for talking to me, I never knew, The Voice of the Rain can be
that soothing!
You know what?
Your pitter-patter sound is calming!
Thank you for healing my soul!
Your petrichor opens the way to my congested heart,
That's probably your art!
And with that, I'd like to fill up all of my empty carts!

Upon knowing life is a pain in disguise,
You sat down, selflessly by my side!
You didn't let anybody notice my tears,
Though they are what I often wear,
The bliss of solitude is what I can no longer bear!
A true friend like you can probably help me up a gear!
Yes, I don't fear, when you are here!
Though problems in my life are no longer mere,
You are here, listening to what makes me fear!
Oh dear, Thank you for being my peer!
Honestly, I have lost count of all I have lost in life!
Now, I cry with my eyes dry,
But, I still give every challenging task a try!
Come Rain, let's sign a deal, for you're the one, who provides me with a
better feel,
Yes, I'll kneel if you promise to peal off, darkness and pain underneath,
and make me heal...
So that, better is what I can feel!
So that, better is what I can feel!

7. Oh, Teacher!

You paid heed
when I was in need,
sowed me, when I was a young seed
you never let weeds
irk me with their annoying deeds, and
never let me thrive with ideas of greed,
you never discriminated on the grounds of creed,
helped every child succeed,
you never sounded mean, and
were always keen,
helping every child
you were seen,
Oh, Teacher!
You are doubtlessly a Queen!
I never fear, when
I see your footsteps come near, and then
All I hear is :
"Dear you need not fear"
You just try to up a gear!
you've taught me not to steal,
and mind my deal.
you have always guided me to finish my meals.
Pupils' hearts are what you eternally heal.
Oh, Teacher!, your decals,

will help me sign my future deals.

8. Failures, The Pillars To Success

Failures are the pillars to success,
They are made not to feel ,
bad or depressed .
They are made to hit us, as
The harder they hit us ,
The higher we rise.
Our failures are our ,
constant companions,
Greatest helpers, and
The heaviest burden
So, aren't they made for taking
little bit of rest,
to sit and think that
have we given our best?
No! because we have failed,
Still, that does not matter,
because it's not just the end
FAILURES are no one to stop us,
from doing the things,
which we have planned for tomorrow.
I very well know that ,
I fell down yesterday,

but I am walking today, and
I will be running tomorrow
Our mistakes are the proof,
that we have tried something new
and so are our failures
Then, it hardly matters,
that how we fell, but
what matters is actually,
how we stood up.
And the ones who fives us the power,
to do so are our failures
and for that ,
I thank my failure today,
because it hit me,
and I want it to hit me ,
much harder tomorrow,
So, that I can rise,
higher and higher, to touch ,
the wonderful sky
No one is yet born in this World,
to stop me from, doing
what I want , and
I am the owner of my thinking , and
My failures tell me that,
They will help me
climb the ladders and the pillars,
Of success
So, I thank my failure ,
for certain help .

The past cannot be changed,
but can be thanked,
Because our failures were the only ones ,
who had the ability and faculty,
to get extraordinary achievements ,
from us, the ones,
who failed yesterday,
to give them the power to,
walk today and run tomorrow
Try , try and try, because ,
failure is not born so powerful, to
Overtake our success
rather, failure is simply
the opportunity to begin again,
with more intelligence,
strength , belief , courage
and the competence,
to beat the FAILURE
and yes, Very True
" Failures Are The Pillars To Success "

9. A Photograph

A snapshot, wherein I was looking at her,

Yes, she's a warrior, unsung!

Her smile is naive

Now, she no longer offers to me; a wave!

For herself, she has a smile; saved!

I was looking at her, while she was looking at me,

Yes, there's something both of us can again; never be!

She made me travel back in time, probably when I was five,

Yes, we underwent a deep Dive.

Showing her sparkling white,

She was holding a big kite,

Yes! she possessed an incredible might,

She pushed me back, towards a great height

And at that time I couldn't hold on to emotions tight,

Yes! I was wearing a big smile!

In two ponytails, my hair was tied,

Happiness stood right by my side,

It made me chuckle as if I were a wide tide!

Sadly I'm no longer five,

I'm now, not afraid of Pitch - Dark sights,

They no longer develop inside me, fright!

Also, I'm now, not afraid of heights.

These days I'm just trying to fetch myself the best sight.

Nowadays, I hold on to emotions tight.

The Night has changed,
But, my smile is what it has caged.
People around appear to be fake,
Advantage of my weaknesses is what they often take.
Helpless is what they even make me feel,
But, with time, everything heals.
Better is also what it makes me feel!
My childish demeanour is what it has, away; peeled!
Sadly, I'll never again be able to kneel to the girl,
Who had always selfless been!
But now she's in her teen, Keen on knowing, how she had earlier been!
Keen on knowing how life she has till date, seen,
without being mean,
joyful she has always been!

10. Dear Friend

When you came,
stars and glitters rained together in my life,
When you came
the path of optimism entered my life,
When you came, the ladders of success,
laid down in my footsteps,
And, when you came,
I learnt how to shine
you enlightened me and,
you sparkled me,
So dear friend,
I want to tell you that,
Although our friendship is very old,
it is as worthy as gold.
Or friendship is like a diamond,
Which no one can break,
even with all his intentions
No matter where we go,
And much the distance between us grows,
You'll always be the moon,
Who taught me how to shine,
and a jewel whose worth can never be determined.
As you are the kindest person, one can ever find!
Dedicated to: Nandini Sharma

11. Trees

I am a tree

please don't cut me

please don't divide me into several parts,

it pains, it pains a lot

my heart screams, when I am separated,

from my family and fellow mates

I am a friend of yours,

a true one ...

and the one who is unique from the others

Neither do I eat the fruits which bear on my branches,

nor I will to taste or smell them

There are hazards of breathing in harmful gases

so I breathe that in, for you

because you are my friends

and I am your caretaker because I care for you

When I dance merrily all around

I bring the rain for you all around

I am the only diamond,

on the Earth which shines from day to night

I just swallow the sun's unwanted rays,

which are harmful to you, my friends

but still .. you don't care for me

I provide you with fruits and veggies,

with shade in the bright sunshine,

and pure, fresh oxygen to breathe
I provide you with my wood,
which you use to make comfortable furniture
and many more things,
But still, you cut me
you don't care for me
you don't think about me
you don't think about my pain
So......
Please have some sympathy for me,
please care for me
because if I will survive
then only you can survive
Please save me please save me

12. The Roar of an Offspring's heart!

My heart has been skipping its own beats for a while,
Do you wanna walk with me: For a mile?
I wanna take you for a ride.
And yes, fetch with myself; my Polaroid.
I wanna show it to heaven,
Because I have been tricked, ever since I was seven!
Beauty lies in her wrist,
wherein she's wearing those sparkling eleven!
She's wearing a ring,
given to her by her her king!
And after looking at her,
Heaven's choir bells have started to sing!
It's such a beautiful night,
Just look at her sparkling white, and tall height.
As quite appealing has become the sight!
I wanna fight,
As the moon is to trying to steal her spotlight!
Is he jealous of her shine?
She has already lit up the sky with the glow in her eyes!
She has already melted the icy- floor,
making my heart roar,
immensely from its core!

Oh, God Heaven! I can just not describe the dress she wore!
A flared fairy blue gown,
that I had brought straight from the town,
To which: even the rain had to bow down!
Trust; she poured into the dress, which she requested wore!
And then..
My expectations are what it tore!
A tender heart, shattered from its core.
Lies; being a child I was always told!
Oh, God!
She is the Heaven Goddess!; Her beauty, I will always adore, always
adore!
Looking at her, I can never feel bored.
Yes! She's a mother of three,
She has set her kids free,
to explore the boulevard and the green trees.
Yes! The Heaven Goddess is a mother of three,
and her first offspring is me!
Her beaut, will always be adored, by me!
Her beaut, will always be adored, by me!

13. Chocolate

For a person who is suffering
from deadly diabetes,
Chocolate is the darkest state of mind,
as he's caged inside the bars,
which pretend to be very sweet,
but the bars are not available,
to him at an ease,
though that's the sweetest,
of the sweet,
he stands on the grave,
Of his dream,
Chocolate attracts him..
but being dark and dim,
it never lets him heal
Oh, Chocolate!
Please don't be too mean......
as you are my,
greedy need..

14. Azadi ka Amrit Mahotsav

India is a diverse land
here we lend a helping hand
we always respect our holy sand, as
it is our motherland
It's a land of sages,
known for its past and bravery for ages.
They came up with the idea of trade
but made Indians their slaves,
discriminated on the grounds of caste and race, but
ended up putting all of us in a cage.
to workers, they gave no wage,
made them work tirelessly for their sake.
Then radicals like Bhagat Singh felt the necessity of rage,
and sensed the need of breaking the cage.
After years of struggle
and constant juggle
India acquired independence,
and finally, Indians were set free!
Now, we proudly celebrate 75 years of Independence; Azadi ka Amrit
Mahotsav!
We're now free, and
live our lives with solace and peace
that too at ease!
We're now bees

and no one can seize,
the Aazadi we seek

15. Dear Teacher!

Dear Teacher!
No matter, where I go
and how old we both grow,
We'll share the same bond,
and the speciality will only grow.
Because no matter,
how much the distance grows
You and I will be invariably one heart and soul,
No matter what I'll become,
Your teachings are something
I will never let go.
Your place will be always there in my heart
and your teachings will flow in my blood
just like a pure stream
You sowed me as a seed,
but your hard work and dedication,
made me a strong tree.
So dear teacher, thank you
for encouraging and inspiring me,
and for letting out that I am the best,
and whatever I do just satisfies you.
Thank you for being there for me!
you helped me at every step, to
climb the ladder and pillars to success.

You became my sunshine in darkness and,
My monsoon is dryness.
So, Dear Teacher's!
I want to pay gratitude to you
because you were always there when I needed you.
You taught me what is ethical and what is erroneous!
you lit me up like a candle,
Which could never shine alone.
You taught me to burn like the sun,
and shine like the moon.
I promise to bow my head to your teaching!

16. My Family

To be a part of family like mine,
is truly very divine,
where one understands the grief,
of the other, on the most faithful sides,
To be a part of family like mine ,
is really full of pride.
where one laughs on the joke of,
the other, and smiles to share,
the moment of that time.
We call a group of people,
living together a family, only when
one shares his shoulder,
with the other to give him a little time,
and only when the hurt of one,
is shared amongst everyone, and
only when for each other,
our affection arrises.
we laugh, we cry,
we sing, we fight, sometimes
we ignore each other for a period of time,
but we rejoin,
no one has the power to break it ,
no one has the power to break my family,
no one has the power to break my world.

And no one can do it , because
We trust each other, we respect each other's accountability and thoughts
And trust each other
trust comes by itself in a family
and makes the family complete and strong,
Family is gifted to us in parts
joining it is our task with,
the maintenance of unity and happiness.

17. Dear Santa,

On the day of Christmas, we sing,
as the bells, with a jingle, ring!
I know, you fulfil everyone's wishes,
So here's my wishlist.
Both girls and boys should be,
treated equally,
So that they can enjoy the same bliss,
Gender stereotype should no longer be a postulate,
as it is not at all true,
and is vague.
Girls shouldn't fear,
as bearing it, doesn't allow them to up a gear!
While walking on the streets,
there shouldn't be anybody to give them a stare!
Also, they shouldn't be forced to wrap up themselves in traditional wear!
Wearing skirts shouldn't make them feel scared,
as educated people hardly care!
Oh, Santa!
This Christmas make all the streets safe,
Girls must not be put up in a societal cage!
not even in rage.
So, sign this contract of Women Safety on a page,
and gift this to me, Oh, Sage!
As it often concerns a girl of every age, every age!

18. New Year!

New Year !
Sands of time,
rendered fear
and new session,
has appeared,
Let's make some resolutions,
and work hard
in order to make our dreams,
tomorrow's reality,
and work together in peace and harmony
Let's give our best
and let others rest,
as we have to be the
change we want to see in this world
and let others test !
let's shake our legs,
and give this New Year
a contemporary start.
So that we can move apart,
from all the annoying deeds,
we had into been,
and go ahead, rather than being mean.
Let's ring in the New Year,
with all of our good deeds.

Just like every day is a new beginning,
Every year is a new dawn,
with more sunshine and sunlight
topped with blessings and warmth,
let's give it a chance,
as it is a golden charm, but
It's in our moments of decision,
what are destiny is shaped
and how it has to be caked.
A very happy New Year!
which is meant for everybody's sake

19. Diwali: The Magnificent Sight!

A sweet magnificent sight,
plugged with immense delight,
with jewels of gleam on an autumn night,
meant for paying recognition to the might.
As echelons of zillion gleams adorn,
rays of hope are born
As the colours of rangoli explode,
With an exhibition of colours,
the sweetness of sweets,
the fragrance of flowers,
the smoke of scented candles,
brightness of moonlight
the jubilation of sunlight,
purity of our conduct,
along with more duties and
new responsibilities,
Diwali has knocked on our doors
So, it's time to dress up folks.
as it's a carnival of lights,
compressed with optimistic sights
It's a chronological jamboree of myth and mystery,
mention of it is found, in both mythology and history.

All the streets shine,
with candles light.
Diyas are light up in their place,
and rockets vanish without leaving their trace...
Now it's time to spare a moment of thought, and thank God
For all the love we have sought
May lights triumph over darkness,
May peace transcend the earth,
May God shower his blessings on each one of us...
With an echo of holy chants, contentment and prosperity, may Diwali
light up everyone's lives!
Happy Diwali!

20. The Covid Times, (written in 2021)

"Precautions are better than cure"
One, two, three
hands are saying sanitize me
because we are locked in our houses,
as if we are bees
we can't step out of our periphery
else everyone will have to step in a fix
Four, five, six
are saying "Do your bit !!"
Seven, eight, nine
are reminding us of,
visiting doctors online,
whereas ten and eleven,
say follow your passion
and wake up early at seven,
Twelve asks everybody to eat healthily,
so that we can stay wealthy
While numbers upto nineteen are,
teaching us lessons about self-quarantine
Twenty reminds us of paying heed,
for helping the ones in need,
So, let's sow a seed,

and remove the unwanted weed
moreover, let's try to fulfill everyone's needs....
Stay home,
Stay safe...

Thank You, Readers!

It was a wonderful experience, writing **Sink In Ink**. I hope you have enjoyed reading this book. I'm assuming, it didn't make you feel lonely anymore, and was your friend during hard times!

The joy of writing is incomplete without its readers, thank you so much for sparing out time, and contributing to it. It gave me immense pleasure, to share my, thoughts, perspectives, and viewpoints I have towards life.

I will accept suggestions, with open arms! You may write to me. Let's take the journey ahead, commencing from **Sink in Ink**. Let's see where it takes us. Maybe we'll be climbing, swimming, or diving into poetic verses. It's the start of compiling woven thoughts, hoping to bring out the best for you in the near future.

palakpalak655@gmail.com

Acknowledgement

Family Members

Books: The Elixir of Life!

Teachers

School: The Path to Wisdom.